experience hope

The Secret To Your Best Life

Kevin Berry

Contents

Hope For You

Hope is one of the great intangibles in life. You know when you have it, and you know when you don't. You can see when a family, business, or a team has hope. And you can tell when they don't. You can see it in their eyes.

I will never forget the look in a man's eyes when he cried out for help. It was in Lisbon, Portugal, that I walked down an alley with some friends to bring hope to some very desperate people. The farther we walked, the more it became apparent that everyone around me was either selling drugs or doing drugs—everyone! Then I looked down on the ground, and there he was. This man I did not know gripped my heart. He was lying on the ground, shooting drugs into his legs, and that's when our eyes met. With a look of desperation like I have never seen before, he said, "Help me! I haven't always been like this. I had a family and a normal life—help me!" It was clear from the look in his eyes that he was in desperate need of hope.

This need for hope is for more than just those that are addicted to life-controlling substances. Hope is for the person whose life has been derailed from their destiny. It's for the person who has had a loved one leave this life too early. It's for the single parent, the stressed-out business executive, the overwhelmed, overworked, and the overlooked. It's for every person that has been told they have cancer. Hope is for you.

It seems like we are constantly hearing about another terrorist attack, financial crisis, violence and injustice. Add to that the personal challenges that you face in life, and you are in need of a good dose of hope! Here's some good news: when you have hope, your temporary circumstances don't have to become a permanent condition.

....

What if every day of your life could be filled with hope?

....

When you have hope, the sky is the limit. You are willing to dream again. There's a twinkle in your eye. There is a bounce in your step as you walk toward a great future. You start to see all the good that lies just ahead of you. It's like life is being poured into you.

What if every day of your life could be a day filled with hope? What if hope was something that was in your grasp? What if you were so filled with hope that you actually became a conduit of hope to everyone you come in contact with? Is it possible? YES! Hope is the difference-maker, the game-changer for every person... for YOU!

Winston Churchill was asked by a reporter what his country's greatest weapon was against Hitler's Nazi regime. Without pausing, he said, "It's what England's greatest weapon has always been—hope." Through the pages of this little book, I'm going to pour some hope into you. Wherever you are at today, be encouraged. There is hope for you in Jesus Christ.

When Jesus walked the earth, thousands would flock to hear Him. They saw hope in His eyes, heard hope in His voice, and they began to experience hope! They would hang out with Him for days at a time and without food! Why?

They were hungry for something more than food. They, like us, were hungry for hope.

Jesus, who came to the earth as one hundred percent God and one hundred percent man, lived a sinless life. He willingly died on the cross, was buried, and rose from the dead three days later. He paid the penalty for your sin and He purchased hope for you! There's another level of hope that you are about to start walking in. As we spend the next chapters of this book together, things are going to start looking different for you. It's the start of a new day for you, my friend. **It's time for you to experience hope!**

This is my prayer for you:

*I pray that God, the source of **hope**, will fill you completely with joy and peace because you trust in him. Then you will overflow with confident **hope** through the power of the Holy Spirit.*

- Romans 15:13

Chapter 1

Can I Help You?

Hope for when you're feeling stuck

Don't be afraid, for I am with you. Don't be discouraged, for I am your God. I will strengthen you and help you.

- Isaiah 41:10

I went to meet a friend at a local gym to work out, but he didn't show. I decided I'd go ahead and work out anyway. It was pretty intimidating. Most of the guys there had biceps the size of my thighs—they were huge! I reluctantly went to the bench press and slapped some weights on.

Then it happened. I had the weight laying across my chest, but I just could not push that bar up one more time. I was stuck! I laid there thinking about how I was going to get out of this. I could just lean to one side and let the weights fall off the end of the bar, but I didn't want to draw attention to myself. As I continued to explore my options, one of those guys with giant muscles walked up behind me and said, "Can I help you?" I squeaked out a "yes," and with one arm he pulled the weights off my chest. I thanked him and quietly left.

Even though I didn't want people to know that I was stuck under that weight, apparently someone noticed me. Without me even asking, he came to help me. How much more do you think the Lord notices you when you need help? God is the kindest person that I've ever met. He comes to you when you need help the most. In the moments when you don't know what to do, He says, "Can I help you?"

Today, this is what the Lord is saying to you! He is saying, "I know what you are facing. I know what you need help with, and I will help you!" When you look at the task in front of you and it looks bigger than you... when the weight is just too much... the Lord says, "Can I help you? I know how to do that. I can help you! I AM the Lord your helper." It sounds almost too good to be true, doesn't it? I mean, the Maker of Heaven and Earth, the One who holds the world in His hands like it's a grain of sand, would help you? You might be thinking, "Maybe God would consider helping me when I get better?" Hear me, my friend, the Lord doesn't wait for you to "get better" to help you.

When you were at your worst, God sent His best for you!

> *But God showed his great love for us by sending Christ to die for us while we were **still sinners**.*
>
> *- Romans 5:8*

Do you feel stuck in life? Is there something you are trying to carry and it's just too heavy? Have you been in a place where it just seems like you can't get any traction? Or maybe you've even come to the point where you just believe that's the way it will always be. The good news for you today is—from the marriage that is broken, to the broken heart, to the crushed in spirit—there is hope for you.

....

God is the kindest person that I've ever met. He comes to you when you need help the most.

....

It's a new day for you. Hope has finally arrived and is calling you by name. That's exactly what Bartimaeus thought the day that Jesus came to town. Though he could not see at the time, he could hear just fine. He had heard about the miracles Jesus performed—how blind eyes could now see, how crippled people were walking, how those without hope found hope. I mean, that's what everyone was talking about. So when he heard that Jesus had come to town and was walking by, he shouted.

> *"Be quiet," many people yelled at him. But he only shouted louder, "Son of David, have mercy on me!" When Jesus heard him, he stopped and said, "Tell him to come here." Looking at Bartimaeus he said, "What do you want me to do for you?"*
> *- Mark 10:48-49*

Why would the crowds tell him to be quiet? They all knew that Jesus was known for healing people. Didn't they care about Bartimaeus? Didn't they want to see him get his miracle? Regardless of the people yelling at him, I love what he did next! You see, the day that Jesus came to town was the day that he refused to be quiet. It was the day the King of Kings said, "Tell him to come near." It was the day the Lord looked Bartimaeus in the eyes and said, "What do you want me to do for you? How can I help you?" It was the day that a weight was lifted off of him, everything changed, and he could see!

Let me ask you a couple questions: What is it that you would like the Lord to do for you? What miracle do you need in your life?

What an amazing day this is. It's the day when you keep shouting and refuse to be quiet. It's the day that you ask and keep on asking. The day when your heart is filled with expectation. It's the day when you realize that everything can change. The day when you realize that your temporary situation doesn't have to be a permanent condition! It's the day when Jesus looks at you in the eyes and says, "What do you want me to do for you?"

How can you experience the Lord's help in your life? Simply ask Him. It's time to stop trusting in your own efforts. I could have tried all day long in the gym to lift that weight off my chest, but it was just not going to happen. At some point you have to look at God and say, "Yes, Lord, I could use some help here." Hope for you starts with a simple "yes" to the Lord's offer to help. Will you say yes to Jesus today?

*God is our refuge and strength, always
ready to help in times of trouble.*

- Psalm 46:1

Let's pray together: *Father, I thank You that
You are good. I need Your help. There are some
things in my life that I just can't fix. Without
Your help, I'm stuck. I can't save myself and
I need You. Please forgive me for my sins. I
receive Your Son Jesus as my Savior... my hope!
I can't save myself, so from this day forward I
am Yours! I receive forgiveness and adoption
into Your family. You are my Father, and You
love to bless Your kids. You love to be kind to
me. You love to surprise me with Your favor. I
put my trust in You today and my heart is filled
with expectation. I'm expecting Your help today.
Thank You!*

Chapter 2

Ouch!

Hope for when you hurt

When you're in over your head, I'll be there with you. When you're in rough waters, you will not go down. When you're between a rock and a hard place, it won't be a dead end—Because I am God, your personal God, The Holy of Israel, your Savior. I paid a huge price for you... That's how much I love you! (You are precious to me) So don't be afraid: I'm with you.
- Isaiah 43:2-5 MSG

I was out fishing early one morning, enjoying a cup of coffee while watching the steam come off the lake. It was beautiful. Then I felt something hit my line and I reeled in a big pike. I got it in the boat, and somehow in the excitement of the moment, suddenly the lure that was stuck in its mouth went from its mouth to my hand! That was a first for me—ouch!

The barb of the hook went all the way through my finger. I tried pulling it out, cutting off the end of the barb. I even considered taking a pair of pliers and just ripping the hook out like I would if it was in the mouth of a fish, but I couldn't bring myself to do it. All my efforts only resulted in one thing: I hurt even more. One minute, everything was perfect. The next, I was hurting. Sometimes this is the way it is in life. One minute everything seems fine, then out of nowhere—ouch! The pain comes.

Maybe for you it's the loss of a loved one, betrayal, the sting of rejection, words that were said that should have never been said, an injustice, or perhaps the pain of abuse. But somehow, sometime, tragedy came knocking at your door. In painful moments like these, you may be tempted to think, "I believe that God loves me, but I just don't think He likes me." I mean, how could He if all this stuff is happening in my life? I want to encourage you, my friend, the Lord sees your hurt today and He says:

> *When you are in over your head, I'll be*
> *there with you. When you're in rough*
> *waters, you will not go down. When you're*
> *between a rock and a hard place, it won't*
> *be a dead end—Because I am God, your*

personal God, The Holy of Israel, your
Savior. I paid a huge price for you... That's
how much I love you! (You are precious to
me) So don't be afraid: I'm with you.
- ***Isaiah 43:2-5 MSG***

Be encouraged, my friend, you're not alone. You are going to get through what you are going through. There is hope for you in Jesus! And what you're going through isn't happening because God is mad at you. The Lord says, "You are precious to Me." The Lord is always close to the broken-hearted. It is His delight to carry you through the painful times. Remember, Satan (the devil; the enemy), comes to steal, kill, and destroy, while Jesus came to give you life and life to the max.

You are not meant to just survive, you are meant to thrive! Every obstacle you face is actually an opportunity in disguise, an opportunity for you to grow!

. . . .

You are going to get through what you are going through. There is hope for you in Jesus!

. . . .

Have you ever heard of David and Goliath? It would be a fight to the death. A young boy against a giant, and the odds didn't look good. David could never have been known as the giant-killer if he wasn't willing to stand up and fight when no one else would. There is some thriving for you, some victory for you, just on the other side of a fight. The reality is you can't be an overcomer unless you have to overcome some things.

Author Jim Rohn once said, "The greatest value in life is not what you get. The greatest value in life is what you become." And there are some things you will never become without resistance. When things look bad that means it's time to **look up**.

The greatest benefit to the challenges we face is that they cause us to turn to God! If you don't look up to God in prayer, all you can see is the danger but not the deliverance. This was the case with Elisha's right-hand man. He woke up only to discover that they were surrounded by an army.

When the servant of the man of God got up early the next morning and went outside, there were troops, horses, and chariots *everywhere. **"Oh, sir, what will we do now?" the young man cried to Elisha.***

- 2 Kings 6:15

We've all been there haven't we? We see something with our eyes and say, "WHAT WILL WE DO NOW?" Your knight in shining armor has become a nightmare, and you say, "What now?" Everyone has a story, (insert your own challenge here), and God knows your story.

....

Every obstacle you face is actually an opportunity in disguise, an opportunity for you to grow!

....

My friend, Pastor Billy Burke, was told by doctors that he had stage-four cancer and had only months to live. It wouldn't be long before his body would double in size. He had to start treatment now! Tragedy knocked on his door.

The big deal in life is not whether challenges come your way. The big deal is what you do with them. What do you do when it looks like you are out of options? You look up! That's what my friend Billy did. In a very short time, he found himself sitting in his doctor's office, but this time it was the doctor who was shocked. His doctor said, "I have the reports right here that show your body is full of cancer. And I have the most recent reports right here. This is really strange. The cancer is not there now, it's gone! What did you do?"

He did what we all need to do the most—look up to God. Today, look up to God for help, for healing, for peace, and for strength.

"Don't be afraid!" Elisha told him. "For there are more on our side than on theirs!" I wonder what his servant was thinking then. *Really? Well, I'm looking, my glasses are on, I realize I'm not the greatest in math, but it's looking like we are surrounded. There are lots of them and only two of us.*

> *Then Elisha prayed, "O LORD, open his eyes and let him see!" The LORD opened the young man's eyes, and when he looked up, he saw that the hillside around Elisha was filled with horses and chariots of fire.*
>
> *- 2 Kings 6:17*

Now he could see what Elisha saw all along. What a prayer! He didn't pray, "Lord, change the circumstances." Rather, he asked to open his eyes to see the rest of the story! And everything changed. He went from only seeing the danger to now seeing the deliverance. He went from being overwhelmed to being an overcomer. When you look up to God in prayer, it will be a game-changing moment for you.

> *Don't worry about anything; instead, pray*
> *about everything. Tell God what you need,*
> *and thank him for all he has done.*
> *- Philippians 4:6*

Don't worry about anything! If you've been living on the worry channel, it's time to change the channel! It's time to look up to God with a thankful heart! The reality is most of us have a million blessings and only a few problems. The only thing that is clear in your sight is what you focus on; everything else is a blur. So stop looking at the problem and look up to God in prayer. Pray (simply talk to God) about everything... He's listening right now.

In 1952, Florence Chadwick stepped into the waters of the Pacific Ocean off Catalina Island determined to swim to the shore of California.

She had already been the first woman to swim the English Channel both ways. The weather was foggy and chilly and she could hardly see the boats accompanying her. Still she swam for 15 hours. When she begged to be taken out of the water, her mother was in the boat beside her and told her that she was close and she could make it. Finally, physically and emotionally exhausted, she stopped swimming and was pulled out of the water. It wasn't until she was in the boat that she discovered the shore was less than a half mile away. At a news conference the next day she said, "All I could see was fog. I think if I could have seen the shore, I could have made it."

My friend, I want you to see the shore today. I want you to see the victory that is on the other side of this fight. You are not going to just survive this, you are going to thrive. You are going to get through what you are going through. **I want you to see that there is hope for you.**

Prayer: *Father in Heaven, I look up to You. I ask that You will heal me where I hurt. I ask that You will give me all the strength and grace that I will need in the days ahead. Help me to see more than what is right before me... help me to see that You are with me. Help me to see what I'm becoming in this current season.*

Chapter 3

What Are You Thinking?

Hope for when your thoughts are taking you in the wrong direction

Let God transform you into a new person by changing the way you think.

- Romans 12:2

It was a beautiful summer day in northern Michigan where we were on our family vacation. We decided to take a paddleboat around the lake. After quite a while of exploring little nooks and places around the lake, we started to head back. We were out in the middle of the lake, and for some reason we were just going in circles! It didn't matter which way I turned the rudder or how fast or slow we paddled. I soon discovered the problem: a bunch of weeds had collected on the rudder that steered the boat. Our direction was never going to change until I dealt with the weeds.

For many, this is the way life goes. They seem pulled in a direction they don't want to go. Often it's the result of an area of their life they can't see—the area of the mind, their thoughts. Just as I had to clean up the underside of the paddleboat, so we have to clean up the way we think or else our lives are forever pulled in a direction we don't want to go. It's what the Bible calls renewing our minds.

....

You can only upgrade your life to the extent you upgrade your thinking.

....

If you want to walk in a new dimension of hope, you will have to upgrade the way you think. You'll have to begin to choose your thoughts carefully. Here's the thing: you can only upgrade your life to the extent you upgrade your thinking.

Is your life heading in the direction you want it to go? Is your belief system producing what you want in life? Have you tried to break free of past failures and hurts but can't? Why do things seem to repeat themselves in our lives?

My car had some issues a while back. After driving back from lunch, I was walking away from my car when it started by itself! Then it started locking and unlocking the doors and the horn started going off. On the outside, the car looked fine. But on the inside, something in the wiring was messed up, and it showed! Could this be what is happening to you, too? You look fine on the outside, but inside there is some bad programming, some internal wiring that is messed up in the way you think, and it shows itself every once in a while. There are people who repeatedly sabotage their life. The problem is in their mind. They are filled with toxic thoughts that, according to the research of Dr. Caroline Leaf, actually shut their brain down! How does this happen? Often, history has programmed us.

. . . .

Often the biggest obstacle to you walking in a new dimension of hope is... you. It's your mind, the way you think.

. . . .

This is what happens to elephants that have been taken captive. At a very young age when they are only 150 pounds, they are tied with a rope around one leg. They try as hard as they can to get free, but eventually something happens and they stop trying. I've learned that it's at the moment when the young elephant gets down on its knees that its thinking has shifted. It gives up and thinks, *this is how it will always be.* This sticks with them so deeply that even when they are 8,000 pounds and could easily break that rope, they don't. Why? Because of the way they think. They bought the lie that says, "I can't. No use trying. It will always be this way."

For most people, the biggest obstacle to you walking in a new dimension of hope is... you. It's your mind, the way you think. This was the obstacle one dear woman faced until she encountered the extravagant kindness of Jesus. She had lived with constant bleeding for 12 years. She spent all the money she had on doctors but only grew worse. When it came to hope, she was running on empty... that is until she started to change the way she thought.

For 12 years she heard, "What is wrong with you?" "It's all your fault that this has happened." "You deserve this." "You are unclean.

Get away, sinner!" It was common for people of that day and culture to think if someone was sick, it was because they sinned. In other words, it was their fault. If she continued thinking like this, she would never have received the hope she desperately needed. But she started to think to herself, *there is hope in Jesus for me. I can't change my past, but I can change my future.* She now had the great game-changer in life—she had hope!

> *She thought to herself, "If I can just touch his robe, I will be healed."*
>
> *- Mark 12:28*

Is there hope for those that have had the barbs of toxic thoughts sink into their minds? Yes! Your biggest problem is not your boss, it's not your spouse, it's not your parents, and it's not the cards you were dealt in life. Your biggest fight is not with somebody else. Your biggest fight is with the lies that have been spoken to you, the lies and limitations that you have accepted. It's time for a change, it's time for hope, it's time for Jesus to set the captive free! How can you begin to change the way you think today? How can every day of your life be filled with more hope?

1.   **Ask God to help you reject all negative, toxic thoughts.**

What are the lies you have been believing? What are the toxic thoughts that have been rolling around in your heart? We take time to clean out our garage, cars, and our closets. It's time to clean out the toxic thoughts that have become overgrown in your mind and heart—toxic thoughts like: it can never change, that you are stuck, that you don't have what it takes, that you will never be good enough. It's time to accept full responsibility for your own mind and stop blaming others. If you have had negative parents or experiences, they may have created a disposition in you, but not a destiny! You choose! The Lord will help you identify what thoughts you have been believing that will only cripple you and keep you from reaching your full potential.

Remember, Satan is a liar and always has been. He has lied from the Garden of Eden to the Garden of Gethsemane. Jesus said the devil is the father of lies, it's his nature to lie. It's important for you to recognize where those lies you have been listening to are coming from. Demons are on assignment to destroy your life. They come and whisper lies in hopes that you will believe them, get stuck, and go in circles. It's time for you to resist the devil in Jesus' name!

*So humble yourselves before God. **Resist** the devil, and he will flee from you.*

- James 4:7

And the Holy Spirit helps us in our weakness.

- Romans 8:26

2. Ask God to give you new, healthy thoughts.

After years of toxic thoughts, being a public outcast, judged and criticized, something amazing happened to replace those toxic thoughts with healthy thoughts when Jesus called the healed woman, "Daughter!"

And he said to her, "Daughter, your faith has made you well. Go in peace. Your suffering is over!"

- Mark 5:34

She received more than a physical healing. She was being healed of years of lies, hurt, and the resulting toxic thinking in her own life. The word "daughter" is a word of love, endearment, and affection. As babies, we are all born crying for affection. What makes a baby stop crying? Being held in its mother's or father's arms—and we never grow out of that. Trust me, this woman had not outgrown the need for acceptance, affection, and the need to see love in someone's eyes.

....

The most healthy thoughts you can have are the thoughts that God has about you.

....

Did you know God is thinking about you? His thoughts about you are more than can be counted and they are good! He's not staring at your failures, He's looking at your future. Jesus Christ took all your failures on the cross when He was crucified. Scripture declares that He endured the cross for the joy that was set before Him. What was the joy set before Him? You were! Now there's something to think about.

For a list of healthy thoughts that God thinks about you, see the end of the chapter: "You Are Chosen."

Prayer: *Father, I ask You to help me rid my life of all toxic thinking. Grant me the wisdom to guard my life from the kind of thinking that will get me nowhere. Fill my heart with the thoughts You have about me. Fill my heart with hope, and begin to make me a conduit of hope for others.*

Chapter 4

Amazing Grace

Hope for when you fail

*May God give you more and more grace
and peace as you grow in your knowledge
of God and Jesus our Lord.*

- 2 Peter 1:2

It was the 1929 Rose Bowl, the most famous Rose Bowl game in history—Georgia Tech vs. University of California. Roy Riegles picked up a fumble and ran 69 yards. The problem was, he was running in the wrong direction! He was tackled by his own teammate at the three-yard line.

At halftime, nobody said a word. The coach gave a little talk and then said, "Let's go." Roy just sat in his seat. The coach looked at Roy and said, "Roy, let's go." "I can't! I've ruined myself, I've ruined you, and the University of California. I can't go out there to save my life," Roy said.

I love what the coach did next. He looked at Roy in the face and said, "Roy, get back out there. The game is only halfway over!" Roy went on to play the best second half of his life. What was talked about more than his blunder, was his great second half.

I want to encourage you today. God is not through with you! There is no expiration date on your potential! The game isn't over... it's only halfway over. What you are experiencing today is just a paragraph in the story of your life, not the conclusion. If you've ever dropped the ball, if you've ever found yourself running in the wrong direction, or if you've ever made a mistake that you wish you could take back, I've got some great news for you! One moment in God's grace can reverse a lifetime of disgrace. One moment in His extravagant favor can achieve what you could never achieve on your own.

People sing songs about grace, we say grace before a meal, we have a grace period in paying our bills, we believe in grace... but do we really know what grace is? And more than simply knowing what grace is, have you experienced God's amazing grace?

....

One moment in God's grace can reverse a lifetime of disgrace.

....

Grace is favor, specifically favor that you do not deserve, that you did not earn. Grace is so hard for us to wrap our minds around because it is so unlike what we are used to. We grow up hearing things like: The early bird gets the worm; There is no such thing as a free lunch; No pain, no gain; You get what you work for! For the most part, we receive what we achieve in life. But with grace, we receive what God has achieved for us. Grace gives us the hope that our failures are not fatal!

....

For the most part, we receive what we achieve in life. But with grace, we receive what God has achieved for us.

....

We live in a day when people are starved for grace. Several years ago in a stadium in London, 70,000 people gathered for a concert with several bands. For about 12 hours, music groups blasted the crowd with their music. The last act was Jessie Norman. She came to the center of the stage with no band, no music, just Jessie. The drunken crowd started to yell for more of the other bands. Then slowly she began to sing, "Amazing grace, how sweet the sound, that saved a wretch like me. I once was lost but now I'm found, was blind but now I see." The crowd became completely silent. By the second verse the crowd began to sing along. Why? They were captivated by grace. Like so many of us today, they were hungry for genuine grace.

Most of us have had enough of people railing at us, judging us, telling us how messed up we are, and like Roy "Wrong Way" Riegles, we already know we've dropped the ball. We already know that we're not perfect, that we've messed up. What we need is grace. What we need to hear is that it's not over. There is hope for us. That God is not mad at you. That He's the one in your corner saying, "You've got this, there is a second half to still be played. You have a second chance in life and it's not because you are so good and you did everything right. It's because I'm good, I'm gracious, extremely kind, and I love you!" That's what the woman caught in the act of adultery heard the day that she looked grace in the eyes.

> *Then Jesus stood up again and said to the woman, "Where are your accusers? Didn't even one of them condemn you?" "No, Lord," she said. And Jesus said, "Neither do I. Go and sin no more."*
>
> *- John 8:10-11*

The woman caught in adultery earned, according to the law, one thing—death! When Jesus said, "Whoever is without sin, you throw the first stone," the yelling stopped, the stones dropped, and one by one they walked away, from the oldest to the youngest. Jesus being the only one left, stood and said, "Where are your accusers? Where are the ones saying, 'You are not good enough? What kind of woman are you? What kind of mother are you? You'll never be better, you'll never be more than what you are right now—a failure!'" When grace steps in, the accusers have to step off. They have no more game, they have no mud to throw.

> *God sent His Son into the world not to judge the world, but to save the world*

through him. There is no judgment against anyone who believes in him.

- John 3:17-18

God isn't interested in watching you try to change. He is interested in bringing about a change *in* you! Grace always starts in the heart. Taylor Storch was killed in a skiing accident at the age of 13. Her parents decided to donate her organs to help patients in need. Their only request was they wanted to hear the heart of their daughter. So they flew out to Phoenix where a woman named Patricia had received Taylor's heart. They handed Taylor's parents a stethoscope and when they heard the healthy heart beating, they were hearing the heart of their daughter. It was in a different body, but it was their daughter's heart!

When you have placed your faith in Jesus, God hears your heart... and when He hears your heart, He hears the heart of His Son!

It is no longer I who live, but Christ who lives in me.

- Galatians 2:20

And I will give you a new heart with new and right desires, and I will put a new spirit in you. I will take out your stony heart of sin and give you a new, obedient heart. And I will put my Spirit in you so you will obey my laws and do whatever I command.

- Ezekiel 36:26-27

Be encouraged today, my friend. No matter what you've done or where you've been, there is some grace for you today! That amazing grace gives you the ability to know that what you are currently experiencing is only the first half of the game. Then grace gives you the power to get up and go play the best second half possible!

Prayer: *Father in Heaven, I thank You for Your amazing grace. I'm thankful that You express Your goodness to me, not because I'm so good, but because You are good! Your grace has achieved for me what I could never earn: forgiveness, right-standing with You, and the right to be adopted into Your family through faith in Your Son, Jesus Christ! Thank You!*

Chapter 5

Time to Forgive

Hope in the storm

When our daughter Sarah was much younger, we were downtown at Riverfront Park enjoying a city-wide carnival. She wanted to go on one of those rides that twirls you in circles. I don't do those very well, but for Sarah I decided to do it. They locked us into this cage thing and off we went. As the ride was spinning around, I quickly discovered the cage we were sitting in also started to spin... and that's when my stomach started to spin.

I was trying desperately to get the attention of the guy controlling the ride. Every time we would go by him, I would yell, "Help!" Then another time around, "Stop!" He just smiled real big, showing his missing teeth. His response to my desperate cry for help was to turn the ride up even faster! It was horrible! I was stuck on a ride with no hope in sight of getting off any time soon. Have you ever gone through a season in your life that felt like a bad ride you desperately wanted to end? Have you ever had someone do you wrong? Maybe it looks like there is no hope of things changing any time soon for you. That's where God's hope comes in.

Nobody makes it through life free of injury. Like most of us, someone, somewhere, has hurt you. I've sat in a funeral home trying to comfort parents who lost their daughter to a drunk driver. She died because someone drank too much. Part of you has died because someone spoke too much, demanded too much, or neglected too much. Tragedy came knocking on the door of your life and before you knew it, you were on a ride you desperately wanted to end.

....

The hope for all of us is believing there is a God in Heaven who knows how to calm storms.

....

Years ago I watched a movie called "Twister." It's about these crazy people that are running after tornados. While everyone else is taking cover, the storm chasers are putting themselves in harm's way on purpose! No thank you! Today, business executives have found a new way to relieve some stress. For a certain price, they pay to go along with the storm chasers, put themselves in danger, and run after some tornados. Seems to me like that would only add more stress. I don't chase storms and it's safe to say that most people don't. But sometimes the storms we didn't ask for happen anyway.

This is what happened to the Apostle Paul. He was on trial for preaching the gospel and was being transported to Rome. Off they went, and everything seemed to be going as planned until:

> *The weather changed abruptly, and a wind of typhoon strength called the 'northeaster' caught the ship and blew it out to sea.*
>
> *- Acts 27:14*

> *The terrible storm raged for many days, blotting out the sun and the stars, until at last all hope was gone.*
>
> *- Acts 27:20*

Luke records the moment with these words: **all hope was gone.** When it looks like hope is too far away, it's been delayed, held up, is nowhere in sight, and you feel like you are at the end of your rope, that is a horrible place to be! The hope for all of us is believing there is a God in Heaven who knows how to calm storms, knows how to carry us through storms, knows how to enable us to actually walk over and through the storms we face.

Winston Churchill said, "When you are going through hell... keep going!" I would have to agree. If you know what it's like to be stuck on the ride of life and to look for hope, then listen closely! There is hope for you. There are some simple steps you can take that will help.

1. Forgive.

Sometimes we find ourselves in the middle of a storm because of our own poor choices. There are other times that we didn't ask for trouble, but it came anyway, and it's in those moments that we have to forgive. Saint Augustine said, "If you are suffering from a bad man's injustice, forgive him lest there be two bad men." Did you know that your forgiveness from God is directly linked to your act of forgiving others?

Paul could have been like most people and played the blame game. He could have pointed his finger and said, "I told you so." After all, he had warned the captain of the boat about this storm but was ignored. Paul chose to do what we all must do when others put us in a harmful situation—forgive.

> *If you forgive those who sin against you, your heavenly Father will forgive you. But if you refuse to forgive others, your Father will not forgive your sins.*
>
> *- Matthew 6:14-15*

I love the way Jack Hayford put it when he said, "To find hope on a hopeless day, begin by forgiving everyone who seems to be trying to ruin your life." Forgive the people who:

- Misunderstood you
- Intended to hurt you
- Betrayed or violated you
- Have injured you

Have you heard the words of Jesus, when He was hanging on a cross being crucified for our sins? He said, "Father, forgive them for they do not know what they do" (Luke 23:34).

There it is... they don't know what they are doing. It's hard for us to understand that the people that have done wrong to us really don't know what they are doing. They don't know the full impact, the destructiveness, or the degree of the damage they have caused. In light of God's amazing forgiveness toward us, there is only one right thing to do—forgive.

....

"To find hope... begin by forgiving everyone who seems to be trying to ruin your life." – Jack Hayford

....

Forgiveness is not a feeling, it's a choice. It doesn't mean that what somebody else did was right. It just means that you are more interested with moving on in life than being tied to the past.

2. Hold onto the hope of God's Word.

The only way Paul made it through his storm was holding onto something God had said.

Last night an angel stood before me and said, "Don't be afraid, Paul, for you will surely stand trial before Caesar! What's more, God in his goodness has granted safety to everyone sailing with you."

- Acts 27:24

You may never have an angel show up in your home saying, "It's all going to be good." But you do have precious promises in the Word of God that will act as an anchor for your soul! If you don't know what God is saying, you are always at the mercy of what you see.

Let us hold tightly without wavering to the hope we affirm, for God can be trusted to keep his promise.

- Hebrews 10:23

When you hold onto the hope of God's Word, you turn your eyes away from the devastation of the moment and onto your destination! When Paul knew what God had to say, he went from hopeless to hopeful, from fear to faith.

So take courage! For I believe God. It will be just as he said.

- Acts 27:25

....

Your miracle is not based on the size of your faith, but on the size of the One you have faith in!

....

3. Be thankful.

> *"You have been so worried that you haven't touched food for two weeks," he said. "Please eat something now for your own good. For not a hair of your heads will perish." Then he took some bread, gave thanks to God before them all, and broke off a piece and ate it.*
>
> *- Acts 27:33-35*

While the storm was still raging on, Paul was giving thanks! The most powerful time of giving thanks is when things still look crazy, when things still look out of control. But you have a promise, you have hope—the eager expectation that something God has promised will certainly happen! Paul said:

Be thankful in all circumstances.
                              - 1 Thessalonians 5:18

A single dad was going to take his son on his first picnic in the morning and the boy was so excited. The dad told his son that he needed to get his sleep, but the son got out of bed several times because he was too excited to sleep. One of the many times the son woke up, his dad said, "What is it now, son?" to which the boy replied, "I just want to say thanks for tomorrow." I love that! We should live every day this way... filled with so much hope that we find ourselves saying thanks for tomorrow!

Prayer: *Father in Heaven, I thank You that through Your Son Jesus Christ, You have forgiven me. Jesus, would You help me to forgive like You? Help me to look at those who have done me wrong in the same way You looked at the soldiers that were nailing You to a tree—like people who don't really know what they are doing. I choose to take all my pain, all that has been done wrong to me, and put it at the foot of the cross. And I release forgiveness to those that have hurt me. I thank You that I'm free, not tied to the past, I'm moving forward with You! Thank You for tomorrow, and all the good that is coming my way, just around the corner.*

Chapter 6

You Are Chosen

Hope for how you see yourself

*Even before he made the world, God loved
us and chose us in Christ to be holy and
without fault in his eyes.*

- Ephesians 1:4

As a young boy we had a field right across
from our house where the neighborhood kids
played baseball. I loved to play, but I hated the part
before the game when captains were picked and
they chose their teams one by one. It was horrible
waiting to be chosen. I was normally the last guy
that somebody had to take, but they never really
wanted me. It stinks to be looked over, to feel
invisible, and it's even worse to be flat-out rejected.

I want to encourage you today—you are
chosen. You are God's first pick! Before He made
the world, He picked you!

*God decided in advance to adopt us into
his own family by bringing us to himself
through Jesus Christ. This is what he wanted
to do, and it gave him great pleasure.*

- Ephesians 1:5

Over the years I have heard people filled with questions they should never have to ask. Why didn't my father want me? Why can't I have a family? Won't anyone pick me? What's wrong with me?

I have good news for you: before the foundations of the world were made, God was thinking about adopting YOU! The King of Kings chose you. One of the major themes of God's Word is adoption! Adoption has always been God's ideal plan for you and me. God's plan to adopt us into His family was not an afterthought.

....

Before the foundations of the world were made, God was thinking about adopting you!

....

My mom was adopted when she was about 9 years old. She told me one day, "I'm doubly blessed because I was not just born, I was chosen! I've been adopted twice—once by God, and once by your grandpa." As a young child, my mom's parents faced a tragedy that resulted in my mother being torn from the family she had. Then in the middle of all the pain, the waiting began—the wait to be adopted, the wait to be wanted. Then one day it happened, and my grandpa walked into the room. The Lord saw this day and made sure that not only was my mom adopted, her sister was adopted into the same family. She was desired and wanted. The truth is, she always has been wanted.

The day my grandfather walked into my mom's life, hope came too, and everything changed for her. She went from being homeless to having a home. She went from being without a family to having a family. When Jesus walks into your life and adopts you as His own, you have what we all need—hope. It's the hope that your past doesn't have to determine your future.

Adoption—being chosen—is all about the extravagance of God. You see, God wants to do more than just save you, He wants a family relationship with you! Adoption is the process of taking someone who is fatherless and making them one's child, thus giving them a father, a family, an inheritance, and community.

....

God wants to do more than save you, He wants a family relationship with you!

....

Father to the fatherless, defender of widows, this is God!

- Psalm 68:5

When Renee and I were newlyweds, I would take my guitar into the front yard of our apartment building, call Renee out onto the little balcony, and start to make up songs that I would sing to her. I loved her so much, my thoughts about her came out in songs!

Here's a great thought: God is thinking about you today, and His thoughts about you are good. They are precious, they are more than can be counted. They are thoughts about who you are today and thoughts about your future. They are thoughts that just have to come out as a song.

God loves you so much, He sings about you! The Bible says:

> *He will rejoice over you with joyful songs.*
> *- Zephaniah 3:17*

He loves you so much that He can't get you out of His mind. He's thinking about you even now! I pray your heart will be filled with wonder at the thought that the same God who created the world with His words loves to sing to YOU! He chose you! Some of you are so hungry to be loved. Those who should have loved you, didn't, and those who could have loved you, didn't. You've been left with a broken heart and at times wonder, "Does anybody love me?"

I want you to hear the voice of your heavenly Father say, "Yes, I do!" You see, God's love for you doesn't depend on how good you are or how bad you are. He loves you just the same. His love does not increase when yours does or decrease when yours does.

> *This is love: not that we loved God, but he loved us.*
>
> *– 1 John 4:10*

*But God demonstrates his own love for us in this: While we were **still sinners**, Christ died for us.*

- Romans 5:8

Here's the thing: God choosing you, God loving you, is something you are meant to personally experience again and again. I remember when our grandchildren learned the word "again." I would pick up Tanner as a young toddler and start spinning him around. Without fail he would say, "Again!" So off we would go again. I think he could have kept going forever; I could not. We must experience the Father's love over and over again. We should find ourselves like little kids saying, "Again."

God's love for you is experienced every time you hear the whisper of His voice, each time you look into the eyes of the people that God has strategically put in your life to represent His kindness to you. Every time you see a beautiful sunrise, you can be reminded that He did that for you. He didn't have to make them so beautiful, but He did, and He did that for you!

My Child,

You may not know me, but I know
everything about you.
Psalm 139:1

I know when you sit down and when you rise up.
Psalm 139:2

I am familiar with all of your ways.
Psalm 139:3

Even the very hairs on your head are numbered.
Matthew 10:29-31

For you were made in my image.
Genesis 1:27

In me you live and move and have your being.
Acts 17:28

For you are my offspring.
Acts 17:28

I knew you even before you were conceived.
Jeremiah 1:4-5

I chose you when I planned creation.
Ephesians 1:11-12

You were not a mistake, for all your
days are written in my book.
Psalm 139:15-16

I determined the exact time of your birth
and where you would live.
Acts 17:26

You are fearfully and wonderfully made.
Psalm 139:14

I knit you together in your mother's womb.
Psalm 139:13

And brought you forth on the day you were born.
Psalm 71:6

I have been misrepresented by those who
do not know me.
John 8:41-44

I am not distant and angry, but am the
complete expression of love.
1 John 4:16

And it is my desire to lavish my love on you.
1 John 3:1

I offer you more than your earthly father ever could.
Matthew 7:11

For I am the perfect Father.
Matthew 5:48

Every good gift that you receive comes
from my hand.
James 1:17

For I am your provider and I meet all your needs.
Matthew 6:31-33

**My plan for your future has always been
filled with hope.
Jeremiah 29:11**

Because I love you with an everlasting love.
Jeremiah 31:3

My thoughts toward you are countless as
the sand on the seashore.
Psalm 139:17-18

And I rejoice over you with singing.
Zephaniah 3:17

I will never stop doing good to you.
Jeremiah 32:40

For you are my treasured possession.
Exodus 19:5

I desire to establish you with all my heart
and all my soul.
Jeremiah 32:41

And I want to show you great and marvelous things.
Jeremiah 33:3

If you seek me with all your heart, you will find me.
Deuteronomy 4:29

Delight in me and I will give you the
desires of your heart.
Psalm 37:4

For it is I who gave you those desires.
Philippians 2:13

I am able to do more for you than you
could possibly imagine.
Ephesians 3:20

I am your greatest encourager.
2 Thessalonians 2:16-17

I am also the Father who comforts you in
all your troubles.
2 Corinthians 1:3-4

When you are brokenhearted, I am close to you.
Psalm 34:18

As a shepherd carries a lamb, I have carried
you close to my heart.
Isaiah 40:11

One day I will wipe away every tear from your eye.
Revelation 21:3-4

And I'll take away all the pain you have
suffered on this earth.
Revelation 21:3-4

I am your Father, and I love you even as I
love my son, Jesus.
John 17:23

For in Jesus, my love for you is revealed.
John 17:26

He is the exact representation of my being.
Hebrews 1:3

He came to demonstrate that I am for you,
not against you.
Romans 8:31-32

If you receive the gift of my son, you receive me.
1 John 2:23

And nothing will ever separate you from my
love again.
Romans 8:38-39

Come home and I'll throw the biggest party
heaven has ever seen.
Luke 15:7

I have always been Father, and I will
always be Father.
Ephesians 3:14-15

My question is... Will you be my child?
John 1:12-13

I am waiting for you.
Luke 15:11-32

Love, Your Dad
Almighty God

Chapter 7

Heaven

Hope for your future

Have you thought about Heaven lately? Have you wondered what it will be like? Do you know if you will be in Heaven some day? That's what Dan and I talked about.

Years ago we were in Florida when my daughter said she wanted to go parasailing. I didn't want to go. I have never wanted to go. I've watched it from the beach and it looks like fly fishing for sharks, except I'm the bait. But I agreed, and before I knew it we were about 500 feet in the air when I said, "Sarah, look! That looks like a huge shark." She replied, "Dad, that's our shadow." Oh, I guess I was a little freaked out. I didn't like the heights, I didn't like the sharks that I knew were down there. So when we were done I was thrilled.

Then the guy on the boat told my daughter to get out of the seat but for me to stay on. He explained that there was another guy who wanted to go for a ride and they have to send up two at a time, so they needed me to go again. I didn't want to go with my own daughter, let alone with some random guy I didn't even know. I figured I might as well strike up a conversation just to keep my mind off of how high up in the air we were.

I asked him his name and we made some small talk. Then Dan told me about some friends of his that went parasailing, became detached from the boat, and crashed into a building and died. That is not what I needed to hear. Yikes! I was thinking, "Dan, why would you tell me that?" But the words that came out of my mouth were, "Dan, let's imagine that you and I become detached from the boat and you crash into one of those hotels on the beach and die. What would happen to Dan?" He said, "Oh, I would go to Heaven." I said, "Great, but how do you know you'll go to Heaven?" I'll never forget what he told me. He said, "Well, I've done a lot of the right things. I try to do good, and I hope that is enough."

As the guys on the boat started bringing us back down, I had a short amount of time to tell Dan that he was working on the "works plan" and the problem with that plan is it never works. Who could ever be good enough in their own efforts to enter Heaven with a Holy God? The answer: nobody. But here is what we can do: we can get on the "grace plan." We can put our trust not in how good we are, but in how good Jesus is. The grace plan is trusting in the sacrifice of Jesus for the payment of our sins—His death, burial, and resurrection!

> *God saved you by his grace when you believed. And you can't take any credit for this, it is a gift from God.*
>
> *- Ephesians 2:8*

I walked across the beach that day and realized that the world is full of "Dans" who are on their way to a hopeless eternity. They rarely think about Heaven and when they do, they think it's something they can earn, hoping that somehow their good will outweigh their bad.

The bulk of humanity runs around so busy in this temporal world that they never take the time to think about the things that will last forever—people and Heaven. Here's the thing: nothing good ever happens in a stampede! But something amazing can happen when you slow down and take a close look at the things that matter in life, the things that will last forever. I invite you to take a few minutes with me in this chapter to slow down and take a look at Heaven. Let your heart be filled with the hope of eternity with God. You just may discover that Heaven is nothing like you thought it was.

> *Since you have been raised to new life with Christ, set your sights on the realities of heaven, where Christ sits in the place of honor at God's right hand. Think about the things of heaven, not the things of earth.*
> *- Colossians 3:1-2*

Arthur Stace was born into a life of poverty at the turn of the century in Sydney, Australia. As a child of alcoholics, he learned at a young age to steal just to survive. As a teenager he became an alcoholic and was in jail by age 15. But all that changed when he met Jesus in 1930. Soon afterward, he heard his pastor cry, "I wish I could shout eternity through all the streets of Sydney." Something gripped Arthur's heart and he wanted to make that a reality. He wanted everyone to think about what would last forever.

He would wake up each morning and for hours write one word, "ETERNITY" about every 100 feet on the sidewalks of Sydney. He did this for years. It's estimated that the man who could hardly write his own name, wrote the word "ETERNITY"

500,000 times and was known as the mystery preacher. Nobody knew who did this until 1956. An architect put "ETERNITY" in copperplate in the Sydney Square. To honor Arthur, in the year 2000 they put "ETERNITY" on the Sydney Harbor Bridge in a fireworks display. Four billion people saw the word "ETERNITY" as they watched the opening ceremonies of the Olympics in Australia.

Eternity gripped the heart of a simple man who had the inward reality of being born again. I pray the reality of eternity will grip your heart today. For some, they hear of Heaven and picture lots of fluffy clouds and a few flying baby angels with harps. Hey, Heaven isn't boring, it's breathtaking! What did Jesus tell us about eternity?

1.   Heaven is a real place.

I'm going to prepare a place for you.
                                    - John 14:2

Some think Heaven is something you create every day around you, as if Heaven is just a state of being but not a real place! Some think Heaven must be boring... singing songs all day long, floating around on clouds, and playing harps. The Heaven spoken of in the Bible is anything but boring!

Someone said, "I pity the man that never thinks about Heaven." Perhaps it should be said, "I pity the man that never thinks *accurately* about Heaven!"

The first time I went snorkeling, I was blown away by what I saw—the fish with beautiful colors and in all different sizes, and the huge stingrays with spots all over them. It was breathtaking! I was seeing things I had never seen before. Our daughter was with us snorkeling in Hawaii and she popped up out of the water and said, "Dad, there's fish down there!" It's not that she didn't know there were fish in the ocean, she had just never seen fish like that before. Heaven is buzzing with activity, beauty, and wonder. You are going to see things you've never seen before. The Apostle Paul said:

> *I do know that I was caught up to paradise and heard things so astounding that they cannot be expressed in words, things no human is allowed to tell.*
> *- 2 Corinthians 12:3-4*

What makes Heaven so desirable, so irresistible? It's not the streets made of gold, the glass seas, or the lack of tears, cancer, pain, war, injustice, hatred, and hurt. It's not even the mansions.

It's *Who* is there that makes Heaven so desirable for me—God the Father, Jesus Christ the Son, God the Holy Spirit! The One who would rather die for me than live without me—He is there!

2.   You were made for more than this world.

I'm going to prepare a place... for you.
- John 14:2

C.S. Lewis said, "If I find in myself a desire which no experience in the world can satisfy, the most probable explanation is that I was made for another world."

I met a man a while back, in of all places, a public bathroom. I didn't know him, and he didn't know me. He looked at me and said, "Tell me there is more to this life. Tell me there is more to life than waking up, eating food, going to work, going home, then doing the same thing the next day. There just has to be more." He was searching for something more than what he was experiencing. Something inside of him knew he was made for more. I was able to tell him about the hope of a relationship with God that he was created for. And the hope of another place that was created for him... and for you!

Animals have a homing instinct. Did you hear about the dog that walked all the way from Colorado to California to find his family? We too have a homing instinct in our soul. Our heart's deepest desire and longing is to come home where we belong. Our hearts long for more than what we see every day. We long for something better, for a place where there truly is peace and joy, where every tear is wiped from our eyes, a place where there is no more pain. Solomon tells us that, "eternity has been placed in the heart of every man" (Ecclesiastes 3:11).

The fact is we have been created for another world, to experience a life-giving relationship with God the Father! Jesus came to give us life and life more abundantly... life to the max today! That means we get to experience a little bit of Heaven today.

For this world is not our permanent home;
we are looking forward to a home yet
to come.

- Hebrews 13:14

If our hope in Christ is only for this life,
we are more to be pitied than anyone in
the world.

- 1 Corinthians 15:19

3. He's coming back.

*When everything is ready... I will come
and get you so that you will always be with
me where I am.*

- John 14:3

Did you hear the desire of God's heart in
that? He wants to be with you! He's coming back
for you. Why did Jesus go to the cross? Why was
He resurrected from the dead? It was all for relationship with you. The same Jesus that came as a
little baby is very soon coming back as the King
of Kings.

In 1989, an earthquake in Armenia flat-
tened the nation and killed 30,000 people in just
four minutes. Moments after the deadly tremor,
a father raced to the elementary school to save
his son. When he arrived he discovered that the
building was completely leveled, it was nothing
but a mass of stones and rubble. But he remem-
bered the promise he made to his son earlier that
day, "No matter what happens, I'll always be there
for you."

He found the area that looked like where his
son's class should have been and started to pull
back the rocks. Other parents gathered, sobbing

for their children. They told the man, "Stop! It's too late. You know they are dead, you can't help!" Even a police officer encouraged him to stop. But the father refused. For eight hours, then sixteen, then thirty-six hours he dug. His hands were bloodied and raw... then finally, after thirty-eight hours, he pulled back a boulder and heard his son's voice. He called to his son and heard, "Dad, it's me!" When he got to his son, the boy said, "I told the other kids not to worry. If my Dad was still alive, he'd save me. And when he saved me, they'd be saved too... because you promised, 'No matter what happens, I'll always be there for you!'"

A father would not let a bunch of rubble come between himself and his son. Father God would not allow sin to come between Him and us! The reality is we have all been trapped in sin. When sin entered the world, it was like an earthquake that brought devastation to all of mankind. Sin has destroyed marriages and families. It has destroyed bodies and plagued people's minds with guilt and shame. We had no ability to fix the sin problem.

Like the kids stuck under the weight of their collapsed school, we need someone to save us! So God sent Jesus into this world. He came as a little baby, one hundred percent God and one hundred percent man. He lived a sinless life and then willingly went to the cross to pay the penalty for our sins. Three days later the stone over His tomb was rolled away and He was raised from the dead. God has a history of rolling stones away.

There is one thing disturbing about Heaven, and that's the sad fact that not everyone will be there. Nobody likes to talk about Hell, but it is a very real place. Hell was never created for mankind. It was created for the devil and the fallen angels. In fact, God went to great lengths to make sure that mankind would never see Hell. It was the cost of His Son Jesus. He endured Hell so you wouldn't have to. He rose from the dead so you can live! The only way a person can end up in Hell is to reject God's way of freeing you from that place.

During an edition of 60 Minutes, Dan Rather interviewed Jack Welch, the former CEO of General Electric. At the end of the interview, Dan Rather asked Welch, "What's the toughest question you've ever been asked?" Welch replied, "Do you think you'll go to Heaven?" When asked how he answered that question Welch said, "It's a long answer but if caring about people, giving your all, if being a friend counts, I think I've got a shot.

But I'm in no hurry to get there and find out any time soon."

My friend, you don't have to *think* you have a shot. You can receive Jesus today and *know* that you have a home in Heaven in the future, as well as start experiencing some of Heaven today! You see, it's not so much what you are saved out of, as much as what you are saved into—a close, intimate relationship with the God of the universe.

I have written to you who believe in the name of the Son of God, so you may know you have eternal life!

- 1 John 5:13

Again Jesus said, "The message that will be proclaimed is that there is forgiveness of sins for all who repent!"

- Luke 24:47

Forgiveness is not automatic, it must be received! Will you receive forgiveness today and experience hope?

Prayer: *Dear God, I thank You for sending Your Son Jesus to Earth to live, to die, and to be raised from the dead for me. He gave His life for me, so today, I give my life to You! All that I am, all that I hope to be, I belong to You now.*

Forgive me for every wrong thing that I have ever done. Please take away all the guilt and shame as I receive the gift of forgiveness through the blood of Jesus Christ.

I invite Your Holy Spirit to fill me and lead me forward in a life that will put a smile on Your face. Thank you for adopting me into Your family and giving me a brand new start in life, beginning right now! Amen.

Chapter 8

A Carrier of Hope

Hope for someone else

I was at St. Vincent Catholic Charities and noticed a sign that caught my attention. It was a quote from Mother Teresa that said, "Be the living expression of God's kindness; kindness on your face, kindness in your eyes, kindness in your smile, kindness in your warm greeting." Oh, that we would all slow down enough to show some kindness, that we would be the living expression of God's kindness to somebody today.

The reality is nobody should have to look farther than you to receive hope. If you have received Jesus as your Savior, you have hope inside of you. You have freely been given hope, now it's your turn to become a carrier of hope. Someone said, "A person all wrapped up in himself is a mighty small package." We were never intended to be self-absorbed people. What if you could represent the Father's heart to someone today? What if your kindness could trigger hope in somebody? What if your love could save somebody's life?

The first funeral that I ever officiated was for a 15-year-old girl who had been shot in the head, execution-style. She had run away to Detroit with an older "boyfriend," where she found herself caught in the middle of a drug deal that went bad. I tried to stay strong during the funeral service because that's what I was supposed to do. But when it was over... so was I. When I was by myself, I erupted in tears.

A thought filled my heart—*what if this little girl would have known that she was loved? What if she was able to meet somebody who knew how to love people the way Jesus did?* Oh, that she would have experienced the outrageous love of God. It's possible she would have never run away with this older man pretending to be a boyfriend. It's possible that she would be alive today. It's possible that God could use you to be a carrier of hope!

Every day we have ordinary things we have to do. We have to pay the bills, get groceries, make house payments, go to work. Why not get intentional about doing something heroic, something that has some eternal worth to it, something for someone else, something for someone God deeply loves? The fact is you have never locked eyes on another human being who does not matter to God.

Jesus put it this way:

You're here to be light. God is not a secret to be kept. By opening up to others, you'll prompt people to open up with God, this generous Father in heaven.
- Matthew 5:14, 16 MSG

Give as freely as you have received.
- Matthew 10:8

Heidi Baker gives out Christmas gifts to the thousands of children in her orphanage in Mozambique, Africa. One year, each of the children received a candy bar. She watched as a young toddler who had never even seen a candy bar before, let alone tasted one, took his first bite. The most amazing thing happened. He immediately began breaking it into pieces and giving it away just as fast as possible to the other children around him. As freely as he received, he gave. Will you do the same?

My prayer for you: Father, thank You for the privilege to pray for the child of Yours that has read this book. I'm asking that You would fill them with hope! Lord, You know what they have gone through, the hurts they have had that, in some cases, nobody else knows about, but You do. You have collected every one of their tears. Nothing has escaped Your watchful, loving eyes. I ask You to heal them where they hurt. I ask in the powerful name of Jesus that You would draw them into a close, intimate, life-giving relationship with You. Lord, would You not only give them hope, will You make them a carrier of hope, a carrier of Your presence everywhere they go? I ask this and speak it as a blessing in the name of the Father, the Son Jesus Christ, and the Holy Spirit. Amen.

A Prayer to Experience Hope

Prayer: Dear God, I thank You for sending Your Son Jesus to Earth to live, to die, and to be raised from the dead for me. He gave His life for me, so today, I give my life to You! All that I am, all that I hope to be, I belong to You now.

Forgive me for every wrong thing that I have ever done. Please take away all the guilt and shame as I receive the gift of forgiveness through the blood of Jesus Christ.

I invite Your Holy Spirit to fill me and lead me forward in a life that will put a smile on Your face. Thank you for adopting me into Your family and giving me a brand new start in life, beginning right now! Amen.

Friend, by saying this prayer from your heart, you've been given a brand new start in life, and that is something to celebrate!

Count on it—that's the kind of party God's angels throw every time one lost soul turns to God.

- Luke 15:10 MSG

That's right—all of Heaven throws a massive party every time one person comes to Christ. I celebrate with all of Heaven over you and say a heartfelt, "Congratulations!" on your decision to experience the hope and love that only Jesus can give.

I've written another short book called "The Journey" that is a simple, yet powerful tool to guide you on this great adventure of getting to know your heavenly Father. It's a journey that will change the rest of your life!

To download your free copy of "The Journey," simply go to mounthopechurch.org/thejourney.

Again, congratulations on your decision to follow Jesus. May you truly experience His love, joy, and hope!

the JOURNEY

your adventure **begins...**

When you gave your life to Christ, you started a journey. It's my desire that this book will be a simple, yet powerful tool to guide you on your spiritual adventure of getting to know your heavenly Father. It's a journey that will change the rest of your life!
–Kevin Berry

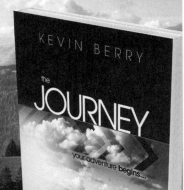

Get a FREE digital copy of Kevin Berry's book. Download your copy today at www.mounthopechurch.org/thejourney

Mount Hope Church | www.mounthopechurch.org

Notes

Introduction

Maxwell, John C. The Maxwell Daily Reader: 365 Days of Insight to Develop the Leader Within You and Influence Those Around You. Nashville, TN: Thomas Nelson, 2007.

Chapter 2

Rohn, Jim. Art of Exceptional Living. Chicago, IL: Nightingale-Conant, 1994.

Burke, Billy. As told to the author by Billy Burke in 2015.

Ware, Susan, and Stacy Lorraine. Notable American Women: A Biographical Dictionary Completing the Twentieth Century. Cambridge, Mass: Belknap, 2004. Viewed at Google Books.

Chapter 3

Leaf, Caroline. Who Switched off My Brain?: Controlling Toxic Thoughts and Emotions. Inprov, 2009.

Chapter 4

Yancey, Philip. What's So Amazing About Grace? Sydney: Strand Pub., 2000.

Lucado, Max. More Than We Deserve, Greater Than We Imagine. Nashville, TN: Thomas Nelson, 2012.

Chapter 5

Churchill, Winston. "Winston Churchill Quotes." Brainy Quote. Xplore.

Saint Augustine. "Saint Augustine Quotes." Brainy Quote. Xplore.

Hayford, Jack. Hope for a Hopeless Day: Encouragement and Inspiration When You Need It Most. Ventura, CA. Regal, 2007.

Chapter 6

Adams, Barry. "A Father's Love Letter." Used by permission of Father Heart Communications, 1999.

Chapter 7

Bevere, John. Driven by Eternity: Making Life Count Today and Forever. New York: Warner Faith, 2006.

Lewis, C.S., Mere Christianity. New York: MacMillan Pub Co., 1952.

Lucado, Max. When Christ Comes: The Beginning of the Very Best. Nashville: Word Pub., 1999.

"60 Minutes." 60 Minutes. Mar. 30, 2005. Television.

Chapter 8

Baker, Heidi. Compelled by Love. Lake Mary, FL: Charisma House, 2008.

Notes